Mercè Segarra / Annabel Spenceley

Bible
STORIES
for Little Catholics

RP
REGINA PRESS
New Jersey

THE OLD TESTAMENT

- Creation, **4**
- Adam and Eve, **6**
- Building the Ark, **8**
- Flooding on the Earth, **10**
- Abraham and Sarah, **12**
- Isaac, **14**
- Esau and Jacob, **17**
- Joseph, **18**
- Joseph and His Brothers, **20**
- Joseph in Egypt, **22**
- The Israelites in Egypt, **24**
- Moses, **26**
- God Talks to Moses from a Burning Bush, **29**
- Leaving Egypt, **30**
- God Makes a Path through the Water, **32**
- God Gives His People Bread, **34**
- The Ten Commandments, **37**
- The Ark of the Covenant, **38**
- The Trumpets at Jericho, **41**
- Naomi and Ruth, **42**
- Samuel, **44**
- David and Goliath, **47**
- Solomon, **48**
- Daniel and the Lions, **50**
- Jonah and the Whale, **52**

THE NEW TESTAMENT

- An Angel Visits Mary, **54**
- Jesus' Birth, **56**
- Good News, **58**
- The Three Wise Men, **61**
- Jesus in the Temple, **62**
- Jesus' Baptism, **64**
- Jesus' Apostles, **67**
- The Wedding at Cana, **68**
- Jesus Feeds a Large Crowd, **70**
- The Parables, **72**
- The Lost Sheep, **75**
- The Growing Seed, **76**
- The Two Houses, **78**
- Jesus and the Children, **81**
- Toward Jerusalem, **82**
- Judas Betrays Jesus, **84**
- The Last Supper, **86**
- The Garden of Gethsemane, **89**
- The Crucifixion, **90**
- The Resurrection, **92**
- After the Resurrection, **94**

Creation

God created the world one step at a time. First, He created day and night, and then the sky, the land, the sea, trees, and flowers. Then He also created the sun, the moon, and the stars. He made all the animals too and, finally, people, so that they would love each other and the earth.

I WILL RESPECT AND TAKE
CARE OF ALL OF GOD'S CREATION.

Adam and Eve

Adam and Eve were the first man and the first woman. God gave them a beautiful place to live: the Garden of Eden. He told them they could eat the fruit of all the trees, except for the tree of knowledge of good and evil in the middle of the garden. One day, a clever snake told them how good that fruit was and that they should try it. Adam and Eve were tempted and ate it. God knew they disobeyed Him, and He sent them out of Eden.

I WILL LISTEN TO MY PARENTS BECAUSE
THEY WANT WHAT IS BEST FOR ME.

Building the Ark

Many years went by and the earth filled with people. Sadly, they had forgotten about God. There was only one good man—Noah—and God told him to build a giant boat, called an ark. God told Noah that it would rain and rain on the earth. The land would flood, but he and his family and one pair of every animal in the world would be saved on the ark.

I WILL WORK HARD TO DO WHAT ADULTS ASK ME TO DO.

Flooding on the Earth

After Noah, his family, and the animals were all on the ark, it rained for 40 days and 40 nights without stopping. Everything was covered with water, but they were safe. Many weeks later, the water dried up and they all could get off the ark. God made a rainbow in the sky as a promise that He would never destroy the earth again.

WHEN I SEE A RAINBOW, I WILL THINK ABOUT GOD'S GOODNESS.

Abraham and Sarah

Abraham and Sarah were married and wanted children very much, but they never had any. One day, God told Abraham to move and live somewhere else. Abraham trusted in God and obeyed Him. He then traveled with Sarah and their possessions to a strange land.

I WILL TRY HARD TO TRUST
THE PEOPLE WHO LOVE ME.

Isaac

One night, God told Abraham that He would give him the new land he traveled to. This land would be for him and his children. Abraham asked God how that would be possible because he was already old and did not have children. Then God told Abraham to look at the stars and said that he would have a family as many as the stars. God kept His promise: He gave Abraham and Sarah a son they named Isaac.

WHEN I AM SAD, I WILL LOOK AT THE STARS AND THINK OF SOMETHING HAPPY.

Esau and Jacob

Isaac and his wife, Rebecca, had two sons, Esau and Jacob. Even though they were twins, they were very different.

After Jacob grew up, he went to live with his uncle. The trip to his uncle's house was very long. One night, he stopped in the countryside to rest and fell asleep with his head on a rock. That night, he dreamed of a staircase that went up to heaven, and Angels went up and down the stairs. God appeared to Jacob and told him that He would give him many lands and many sons, and that He also would protect him.

I WILL SHOW HOW GRATEFUL I AM FOR THE LOVE AND CARE THAT MY PARENTS GIVE ME.

Joseph

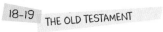

Jacob had 12 sons. The youngest was named Joseph, and he was his father's favorite. His brothers were jealous of him because their father loved him so much and had given him a fine tunic.

I WILL NOT FEEL JEALOUS IF OTHERS DO SOMETHING BETTER THAN I DO.

Joseph and His Brothers

One day, his brothers were watching the sheep. Joseph went to look for them. When he found them, they took the tunic their father had given him. Then they sold Joseph to traders who took him to Egypt, a faraway country.

I WILL TRY TO BE GOOD AND LOVING TO MY BROTHERS AND SISTERS.

Joseph in Egypt

While Joseph was in Egypt, God protected him and gave him the gift of explaining what people's dreams meant. Pharaoh, the king of Egypt, had two dreams and ordered his men to bring Joseph to him to explain them. He said the two dreams meant that Egypt would have good harvests and plenty of food for seven years. Then there would be seven years when little would grow and the people throughout Egypt would not have enough to eat.

Joseph told Pharaoh to store food during the seven good years so that he could feed his people during the seven hard years.

BEFORE DOING SOMETHING, I WILL THINK ABOUT WHETHER IT IS THE BEST THING I CAN DO.

The Israelites in Egypt

Years later, another Pharaoh ruled Egypt, and he had never met Joseph. This new king was afraid of the great number of Israelites living in Egypt, so he decided to make them his slaves. Pharaoh also ordered his soldiers to throw every newborn Israelite boy into the Nile River.

I WILL PRAY TO GOD THAT ALL PEOPLE HAVE GOOD HEARTS.

Moses

An Israelite woman had a son
and, to save him, she put him
in a basket. Then she placed
the basket among tall plants at
the edge of the Nile River. She
had her daughter watch to see
what would happen to the baby.
Pharaoh's daughter found him
and decided to keep him and take
care of him as if he were her own.
This baby was named Moses.

WHEN I PRAY, I WILL
ASK GOD FOR GOOD THINGS.

God Talks to Moses from a Burning Bush

When Moses grew up, he found out he was an Israelite. One day, he protected another Israelite from an Egyptian who hit him. Then Moses was afraid of Pharaoh, so he decided to run away.

Sometime later, Moses was taking care of sheep in a new place. He saw a burning bush nearby, and the voice of God came out of it and told him: "Go back to Egypt and tell Pharaoh to let the Israelites leave." Moses obeyed God, but Pharaoh did not want to listen to him.

I WILL BE BRAVE AND STAND BY MY FRIENDS WHEN OTHERS ARE MEAN TO THEM.

Leaving Egypt

Pharaoh did not want to free the Israelites, so God sent ten plagues—bad things like frogs and biting insects and storms—to Egypt. Pharaoh realized the power of God and finally let them leave. Moses guided God's people toward the Promised Land.

WHEN I PLAY WITH
MY FRIENDS, I WILL
NOT MAKE THEM DO
WHAT I WANT TO DO.

God Makes a Path through the Water

Pharaoh changed his mind about letting the Israelites go and ordered his soldiers to chase them. The Israelites came to the sea and were afraid because they had no boats to cross it. God sent a strong wind and made a dry road with big walls of water on both sides. Then the Israelites crossed the sea.

When Pharaoh's soldiers followed the Israelites on the dry land, God saved His people by having the water rush over Pharaoh's army.

I WILL TRUST ADULTS WHEN THEY TELL ME NOT TO BE AFRAID.

God Gives His People Bread

The Israelites lived in the desert during their travels and were thirsty and hungry. Moses asked God for help, and He sent flakes that fell from the sky and covered the sand. The people called this food "manna." It tasted like bread made with honey.

WHEN I EAT, I WILL BE THANKFUL FOR ALL FOOD,
EVEN IF I DO NOT LIKE IT.

The Ten Commandments

Along the way, the Israelites came to Mount Sinai. God called Moses to the top of the mountain and told him the laws His people were to follow. They were the Ten Commandments, and they were written on two stone tablets. The Commandments told the Israelites what to do and not to do to show love for God and their neighbor.

I WILL SHOW MY LOVE TO GOD AND THE PEOPLE AROUND ME.

The Ark of the Covenant

God gave clear directions to the Israelites about how to build the holy chest—called an Ark—for keeping the Ten Commandments safe. The Israelite soldiers followed God's strict rules about guarding the Ark, which went with God's people while they were traveling through the desert. When the Israelites stopped, they put the Ark in a tent. It was a place of prayer and worship to God.

I WILL BEHAVE RESPECTFULLY IN CHURCH BECAUSE IT IS THE HOUSE OF GOD.

The Trumpets at Jericho

After Moses died, God called upon Joshua to lead His people to the Promised Land. The Israelites needed to capture the city of Jericho, but that would be hard to do because it was surrounded by very high walls. God had a plan. He told Joshua their soldiers should walk around Jericho just once for six days. On the seventh day, they were to walk around the city seven times while the priests blew their trumpets and the people shouted loudly. The walls crumbled and the Israelites could enter the city.

I WILL WORK HARD TO FINISH THE GOALS I SET FOR MYSELF, EVEN WHEN THEY DO NOT SEEM POSSIBLE.

Naomi and Ruth

Naomi, her husband, and two sons left their home in Bethlehem because there was less and less food. In time, Naomi's husband and sons died, and she stayed with her sons' wives: Ruth and Orpah. Naomi was very sad and decided to return to Bethlehem. Although both women left with Naomi, only Ruth followed with her to Bethlehem. Ruth would not leave Naomi because she loved her very much.

I WILL SHOW LOVE AND RESPECT TO MY GRANDPARENTS AND OTHER ADULTS.

Samuel

A woman named Hannah wanted to have a son. She prayed to God with great faith and promised Him that if she had a son, she would give him to the Lord to be His servant. God did give Hannah a son, and she named him Samuel. When the boy was old enough, she brought him to the house of the Lord and presented him to Eli, a priest. Samuel lived there with Eli who took care of him, and Samuel helped Eli with his priestly work.

I WILL KEEP MY PROMISES,
EVEN IF IT IS HARD FOR ME TO DO SO.

David and Goliath

God sent the prophet Samuel to a man named Jesse who lived in Bethlehem. He told Samuel that He had chosen one of Jesse's sons to be the new king of the Israelites. God's choice was the shepherd David, Jesse's youngest son. David fought Goliath—a giant in the enemy army—and, with God's help, beat him with a stone from his slingshot.

David was a good king. He made Jerusalem the capital of his kingdom. Even when David sinned, God loved him and forgave him because he was truly sorry.

I WILL NOT BULLY KIDS
WHO ARE SMALLER THAN I AM.

Solomon

When David died, his son
Solomon became the new king
of Israel. Solomon asked God
to make him wise so he could
govern well. God was very happy
because Solomon had asked Him
for something that was good
for others and not for himself.
While he was king, Solomon had
a beautiful Temple to God built
in Jerusalem.

I WILL ASK GROWN-UPS ONLY FOR
THE THINGS THAT I REALLY NEED.

Daniel and the Lions

Daniel was a great prophet who was taken from Jerusalem to the city of Babylon. The king there made a law that for 30 days, no one was to honor any god or man except him. Since Daniel worshiped God, he did not obey the law. He was punished and put into a cave with lions. Daniel trusted God and the lions did not hurt him. The king and his people realized that Daniel prayed to the one true God.

I WILL ALWAYS TELL THE TRUTH, EVEN THOUGH SOMETIMES IT IS HARD AND EMBARRASSING.

Jonah and the Whale

God sent the prophet Jonah to Nineveh to tell the people there to stop their sinful ways. But Jonah disobeyed God and got on a boat to avoid going to Nineveh. During the trip, there was a terrible storm, and Jonah knew the storm was God's punishment because he had not listened to God. Jonah asked the sailors to throw him into the sea. When he landed in the water, a whale swallowed him. He prayed to God while in the whale's belly, and the whale spit him on the land after three days. Jonah then obeyed God and went to Nineveh.

I WILL SAY I'M SORRY WHEN I DO THINGS THAT MAKE ADULTS MAD.

An Angel Visits Mary

Mary lived in Nazareth. One day, the Angel Gabriel appeared and told her God favored her and she would have a Son and name Him Jesus. Mary accepted the Angel's message. She hurried to visit her cousin Elizabeth to help her because she also was going to have a son, whom she would name John. He later would be called "the Baptist" and would help prepare people's hearts for the coming of Jesus.

I WILL BE AFFECTIONATE
AND KIND TO MY FRIENDS.

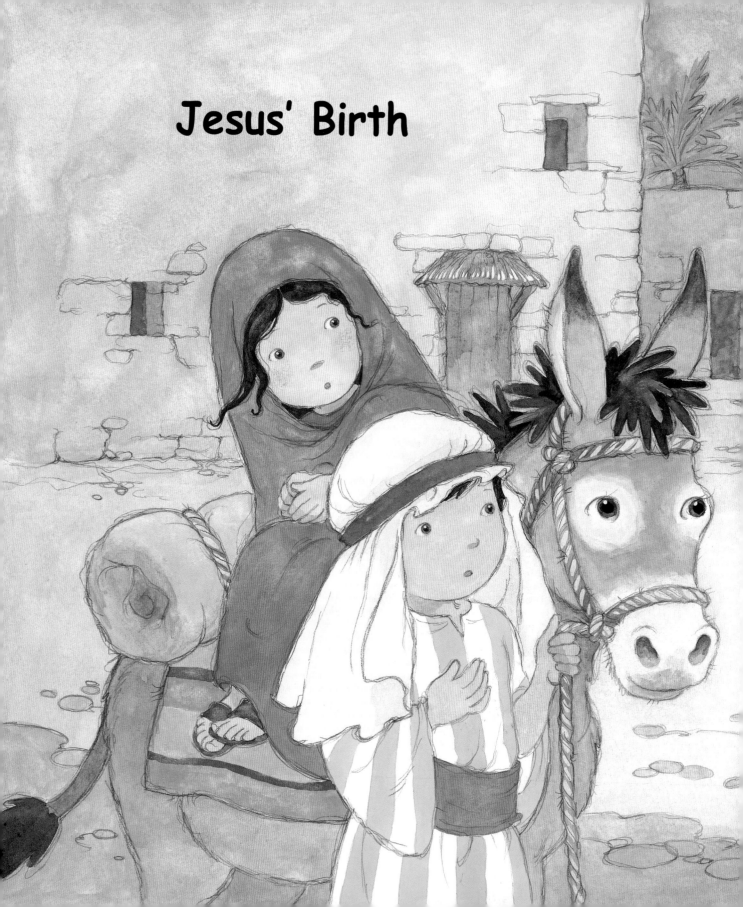

Jesus' Birth

Mary married Joseph, a carpenter. They traveled together to Bethlehem. When they arrived, there was no space for them to stay at the inn. They ended up in a stable among the animals. Jesus was born there, and Mary laid Him in a manger.

I WILL HELP OTHERS WHENEVER THEY NEED MY HELP.

Good News

The night that Jesus was born some shepherds were sleeping in the countryside near Bethlehem. Suddenly, an Angel appeared and a bright light was all around them. The Angel told them that Jesus had been born in a stable. The shepherds rushed to go visit the Baby Jesus.

I WILL DO WHAT MY PARENTS ASK ME TO DO AS SOON AS I CAN.

The Three Wise Men

There were three wise men who lived in the East, a long distance from Bethlehem. One night, they saw a star in the sky and knew it was a sign from God that there was a newborn King of the Jews. They followed the star to Bethlehem and to Jesus. When they found Jesus, they worshiped Him and gave Him gifts of gold, frankincense, and myrrh.

I WILL ALWAYS BE THANKFUL AND VALUE ALL THE GIFTS THAT I RECEIVE.

Jesus in the Temple

Jesus lived with Mary and Joseph in Nazareth. When He was 12 years old, He and His family went to Jerusalem to celebrate Passover. When the festival was over, everyone left for the journey home. At first, Joseph and Mary thought Jesus was among the travelers, and they looked everywhere for Him. Unable to find Him, they returned to Jerusalem and found Him with the teachers in the Temple. These men taught the people things about God, and they were amazed by Jesus' level of understanding.

I WILL EAGERLY LEARN STORIES ABOUT JESUS' LIFE.

Jesus' Baptism

John the Baptist, Jesus' cousin, lived in the desert. He taught the people and baptized many in the Jordan River. Jesus came to the river one day and asked John to baptize Him. After Jesus came up out of the water, a voice came from heaven: "You are My beloved Son." There was no question that Jesus was the Son of God.

WHEN I GO TO A BAPTISM, I WILL REMEMBER THAT JESUS WAS BAPTIZED TOO.

Jesus' Apostles

Jesus started traveling in His country to teach people that God loved them. He also taught them to love the Father and their neighbors. Jesus picked 12 men, some of whom were fishermen, to help Him spread this message. These first disciples of Jesus were His Apostles.

I WILL LOVE OTHERS BECAUSE JESUS ASKS ME TO LOVE THEM.

The Wedding at Cana

Jesus, Mary, and His disciples went to a wedding. During the celebration, the wine ran out and Mary asked Jesus to do something. Jesus changed six jugs of water into excellent wine. This was Jesus' first miracle, and it made His disciples believe and trust in Him even more.

I WILL OBEY MY PARENTS LIKE JESUS OBEYED MARY.

Jesus Feeds a Large Crowd

One day, a large crowd was following Jesus. Most of the people were hungry and did not have anything to eat. He had the people sit. A boy gave Jesus all he had: five loaves of bread and two fish. Jesus gave thanks for the food, blessed it, broke it, and passed out enough bread and fish so all the people could eat all they wanted. Jesus fed at least 5,000 people that day.

I WILL SHARE MY LUNCH
AND SNACKS WITH MY FRIENDS.

The Parables

Jesus would tell stories from everyday life to teach about God's love and forgiveness. These stories were known as "parables." Each story helped people understand how they were to live their lives as God wanted them to live.

I WILL TELL MY FRIENDS ABOUT THE STORY OF JESUS SO THEY CAN LEARN ABOUT HIM.

The Lost Sheep

Jesus told the people the story of a shepherd
who had many sheep, and one day he lost one.
Since that one sheep mattered to him, he left
the flock and went to look for the lost sheep.
When he found it, he was so happy—and he went
home and told his friends the good news.

Jesus told this story to teach people that God
does not want to lose even one of His children.

**I WILL LOOK WHEREVER I CAN
TO FIND THE THINGS I LOSE.**

The Growing Seed

A farmer threw seed onto the ground and it slowly kept growing, even though the man did not understand how. It grew little by little until the crop was ready to harvest.

That is just how Bible stories have helped God's children to grow.

AS I GROW A LITTLE EVERY DAY, I ALSO LEARN NEW THINGS.

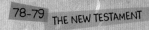

The Two Houses

Jesus said that people who listened to Him and did what He said were like the smart man who built his house on rock. Even though it rained and rained and the wind blew hard against the house, it never fell down because it had strong foundations. A foolish man built his house on sand. What do you think happened to that house?

I WILL LISTEN TO WHAT MY PARENTS TELL ME, AND I WILL OBEY THEM.

Jesus and the Children

One day, parents took their children to Jesus so He could bless them. The disciples told them to go away and not bother Jesus. When Jesus became aware of what was happening, He scolded His disciples. Then Jesus had the children come to Him, blessed them, and said that the Kingdom of God belongs to them.

I WILL COMFORT AND HELP MY FRIENDS WHEN THEY ARE SAD.

Toward Jerusalem

One spring, Jesus and His disciples went to Jerusalem to celebrate Passover. Jesus entered the city, sitting on a donkey. A great number of people welcomed Him by waving olive and palm branches. His arrival caused much excitement because people knew He was the prophet Jesus from Nazareth.

I WILL SAY HELLO TO PEOPLE I KNOW AND BE NICE TO THEM.

Judas Betrays Jesus

The chief priests were jealous of Jesus because He was popular with the people, and they did not want to lose their power. Judas Iscariot was one of Jesus' 12 Apostles, but he betrayed Jesus anyway. He went to the chief priests who gave him money to tell them where they could find Jesus so they could arrest Him.

I WILL NOT FEEL JEALOUS OF OTHERS OR SAY MEAN THINGS ABOUT THEM.

The Last Supper

Jesus knew that He was going to die soon, and He wanted to have His last Passover with the Apostles. He celebrated the first Mass that night and told the Apostles to do the same thing in memory of Him. Jesus also told His disciples to love each other like He had loved them.

WHEN I AM SAD, I WILL THINK ABOUT
ALL THE PEOPLE WHO LOVE ME.

The Garden of Gethsemane

After dinner, Jesus' disciples were with Him when He went to pray in the garden at the foot of the Mount of Olives. Suddenly, Judas arrived with Temple guards who took Jesus to the high priest. He was eventually handed over to Pontius Pilate.

WHEN I PRAY WITH MY FRIENDS, I WILL REMEMBER THAT JESUS ALSO PRAYED WITH FRIENDS.

The Crucifixion

Pilate asked Jesus if He was the King of the Jews, but He did not answer directly. When Pilate tried to let Jesus go, the people said if he did, he was no friend of Caesar. He then handed over Jesus to the chief priests, and they sentenced him to death on the Cross. Jesus died on Calvary, which was just outside Jerusalem.

IF OTHERS ASK ME TO DO SOMETHING BAD, I WILL BE BRAVE AND TELL THEM NO.

The Resurrection

Jesus' disciples buried him in a tomb and rolled a big rock over the entrance. Three days later, women went to the tomb and saw that the rock had been moved. An Angel appeared to them then and told them that Jesus had been raised from the dead. They were filled with joy and went to tell Jesus' disciples the good news.

I KNOW IT IS GOOD NEWS THAT JESUS HAS RISEN FROM THE DEAD.

After the Resurrection

Jesus appeared to His friends at different times after His Resurrection. He told them that 40 days later He was going back to heaven, but He promised to send them a special gift from God the Father: the Holy Spirit. The power of the Holy Spirit would make them stronger in their faith and better able to tell people the story of Jesus.

Ten days after Jesus returned to heaven, His disciples were all together in a room. Suddenly, they heard a strong wind and flames of fire were above their heads. The Holy Spirit was with them! They could now go out and teach as Jesus had taught them.

I WILL TELL OTHERS HOW GREAT IT IS TO BE JESUS' FRIEND.

Bible
STORIES
for Little Catholics

NIHIL OBSTAT: Rev. Pawel Tomczyk, Ph.D.
Censor Librorum

IMPRIMATUR: ✝ Most Rev. Arthur J. Serratelli, S.T.D., S.S.L., D.D.
Bishop of Paterson

The Nihil Obstat and Imprimatur are official declarations that a book or pamphlet is free of doctrinal or moral error. No implication is contained therein that those who have granted the Nihil Obstat and Imprimatur agree with the contents, opinions or statements expressed.

Illustrator: Annabel Spenceley

Author: Mercè Segarra

Original Title of the Book in Catalan: Històries de la Bíblia en 5 minuts
© Copyright GEMSER PUBLICATIONS S.L., 2019
C/ Castell, 38; Teià (08329) Barcelona, Spain (World Rights)
E-mail: info@mercedesros.com   Website: www.mercedesros.com
Tel: 93 540 13 53

Text Copyright United States English Edition © 2019
THE REGINA PRESS
an imprint of Catholic Book Publishing Corp.
77 West End Road, Totowa, New Jersey 07512

ISBN: 978-0-88271-402-8

CPSIA   June 2019 10 9 8 7 6 5 4 3 2 1   G/P

Printed in China
www.catholicbookpublishing.com